GW00854777

Joke tastic

Kids Joke Book : *Try not to laugh!*

First published 2020 by Retro Kid Books
www.retrokidbooks.co.uk
© 2020

ISBN: 9798619519099

Illustrations - Nick Mackie

Dedicated to Taro.
Keep making us laugh.
(and thanks for reading all the jokes!)

Contents

Animals   05

Food   19

Monsters   31

Pirates   45

Crazy World   57

Doctors   71

Knock, Knock   83

School   97

Christmas   109

Movies, Music & TV   121

Animals

What did the squirrel say to the acorn?
'Nice gnawing you.'

Why are bees always buzzing?
They can't remember the words to any songs.

Who is the best singer in the sea?
The tune-a fish!

How can you tell if a rabbit doesn't eat its carrots?
They're the one wearing glasses.

Which fish costs the most at the pet store?
A Goldfish.

What goes zzub, zzub, zzub ?
A bee flying backwards.

What's a cats favourite breakfast cereal?
Mice Crispies!

Why are cows always mooing?
Because their horns don't work!

What do you call a blind antelope?
No eye deer!

Why are there always birds reading in the library?
They love bookworms!

Have I told you about the slippery eel?
'I'd tell you but you wont get to grips with it!'

Why do jellyfish always look scared?
They don't have any backbone!

What game will stick insects never play?
Snap!

8

How do elephants like to travel?
With their trunks!

Which animal loves stormy weather?
A rain-deer!

What do you call a sheep with no legs?
A cloud!

What do you call a duck who eats too many biscuits?
Quackers!

What do you call a donkey with three legs?
A wonky donkey!

How do you stop a rabbit digging in your garden?
Hide your spade!

Where would you find a Lieutenant fish?
In its tank!

What do you call a cat with eight legs that loves water?
Octopussy!

Who is the saddest fish in the ocean?
The Blue Whale!

What do you call a large African animal on a pogo stick?
A Hoppy - potamous!

Which fish love fencing?
Swordfish

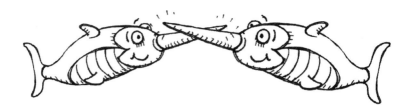

Which seabird is often caught out of breath?
A Puffin!

Where do owls go to prison?
Owl-catraz.

What animal should you never play cards with?
A cheetah!

Guess what a kangaroos favourite game is?
Hopscotch!

What happens when a frog's car breaks down?
It gets toad away!

Why was the spider on the computer?
It was making a website!

What do you call an owl who does magic tricks?
Hoo-dini!

What do you call an alligator wearing a vest?
An investigator.

Why don't crabs like to share?
Because they are shellfish

What do rabbits sing at birthday parties?
Hoppy Birthday!

Why aren't dogs good dancers?
Because they have two left feet!

What do you call two lovebirds?
Tweet-hearts!

What's a dogs favourite instrument?
A trombone!

Why did the girl give her pony cough medicine?
It was a little horse.

What kind of shoes do frogs like to wear?
Open toad.

What kind of jokes do woodpeckers like?
Knock knock jokes!

What kind of facial hair does a moose have?
A moosetash.

What did the shark say after it ate a clownfish?
This tastes kinda funny!

Why do tigers have stripes?
So they aren't spotted.

Fred: **My dog used to chase people riding bikes.**
Tom: *What did you do?*
Fred: **I took its bike away.**

Why are owls good at maths?
They love Owlgebra

Food

Why did the tomato lose the race?
He couldn't ketchup!

How do you make milkshake?
'Shout Boo! at a cow.'

What was Beethoven's favourite fruit?
Ba-na-na-na!

Why couldn't the baker pay his electric bill?
He had no dough!

Waiter what is that fly doing in my soup?
'Swimming sir.'

What does a skeleton order at a restaurant?
Spare ribs!

What birthday cakes do mice like best?
Cheesecakes!

Why was the apple crying?
Its peelings were hurt.

Waiter why is my pizza frozen?
Well you did ask for extra 'Chilli' sir!

Why did the hamburger win the race?
Because it was fast food!

Why did the biscuit go to the doctors?
It was feeling crumby!

How do you make a fruit punch?
Give it boxing lessons.

What do you call a fruit with claws?
A crab apple !

What do sharks eat at parties?

Fishcakes and Jellyfish!

What cheese is made backwards?
Edam.

Heard about the prize winning film about hot dogs?
It was an Oscar Wiener.

Why did the tomato blush?
Because it saw the salad dressing.

What do you call a snack who likes singing Rock n Roll?
Elvis Pretzel!

How did the little girl make a butterfly?
'She threw it out of the window!'

How do you make an apple puff?
Take it to the gym!

What's the best way to make a sausage roll?
Push it down a hill!

Why was the grape unpopular?
Because he was always whining!

What did the mayonnaise say to the potato?
Close your eyes, I'm dressing!

Did you hear about the very ill Italian chef?
He pasta way.

What's crazy and sits on a wall?
A walnut.

Waiter there's a rat in my meal!
Well you did ask for ratatouille sir?

What do you call a sad coffee?
Depresso.

Why was the mushroom so popular at school?
Because he was a fun guy!

What do you give an ill fruit?
Lemonade!

What do you call a fake noodle?
An Impasta!

What do skeletons order at restaurants?
Spare ribs!

What happened when the egg watched a funny film?
It cracked up!

What did the squashed grape say?
Not a lot, it just let out a little wine.

How did the burger propose?
With an onion ring!

What do you call a train made of bubble gum?
A chew-chew train.

What do you call a pig that likes martial arts?
Pork Chop!

Why did the chocolate drop go to school?
He wanted to be a smartie!

What do nuts say when they sneeze?
Cashew!

What kind of key opens a banana?
A monkey.

Monsters : Vampires, Ghosts & Ghouls

What's a vampire's favourite type of dog?
A blood hound.

What do ghosts put on their baked potatoes?
Scream cheese!

What's a sea monsters favourite meal?
Fish and ships!

Which monster gets a half price eye test?
The Cyclops!

Why are vampires always reading letters?
They get a lot of Fang mail!

Why did the vampire visit the doctor?
He couldn't stop coffin!

Doctor, Doctor, I keep thinking I'm a vampire.
Necks, please!

Did you hear about the monster who had ten arms but no legs?
He was all fingers and thumbs.

What do you call a monster with a cold?
The bogeyman!

What is a monsters favourite day?
Chewsday

Where does Dracula keep his savings?
In the blood bank.

What do you call a duck with fangs?
Quackula.

34

How do ghosts open their front door?
They use a skeleton key!

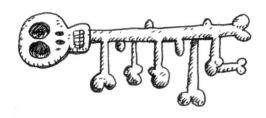

Why are vampires bad at exams?
They always fail the blood test.

What vampire loves eating junk food?
Snackula!

What's a monsters favourite soup?
Scream of Tomato!

Why was the zombie so tired?
He was dead on his feet.

What horse should you never ride?
A Night mare!

How do you stop a werewolf attack?
Throw a stick and shout fetch!

What do you call a tree monster?
Frankenpine!

What kind of music does a mummy like best?
Wrap music

Why are skeletons good at making predictions?
They can feel it in their bones!

Why will a mummy never tell you a secret?
They keep them under wraps!

How do ghosts keep their hair in place?
Scare spray!

What do you call a dancing monster?
The Boogieman!

Why don't werewolves like eating clowns?
Because they taste funny!

What's furry, dangerous and has sixteen wheels?
A monster on roller-skates.

What's black, white & dead all over?
A zombie in a tuxedo!

What do werewolves eat after getting their teeth cleaned?
The dentist.

Why did the vampire use mouthwash?
Because he had bat breath!

Why was the werewolf laughing?
He had eaten a funny bone.

How do you stop a monster from smelling?
Cut off his nose.

What do you always get at the witches hotel?
Broom service!

What do ghosts eat for supper?
Spooketi.

Who did the ghost take to the party?
His ghoul friend.

What do you call a criminal vampire?
A fangster.

Why did the zombie do so well in his exam?
Because it was a no brainer.

Who was the greatest skeleton detective?
Sherlock Bones!

Did you hear about the vampire pianist?
His Bach was worse than his bite!

What is a vampire's favourite fruit?
A blood orange.

Where do mummies go to swim?
The Dead Sea.

What's a monsters favourite dessert?
I Scream!

How do ghosts tell their future?
With their HORRORscope!

What do you get if you cross a vampire with a snowman?
Frostbite.

Pirates

What's orange and sounds like a parrot?
A carrot.

Why do pirates like the sea?
Because its always waving!

Who was the most famous pirate sea creature?
Captain Squid.

Why do pirates enjoy arm wrestling?
They just got hooked on it!

What's a pirate's worst enemy?
Woodworm

Why did the pirate go to the technology store?
He needed to buy a new iPatch!

Why was the pirate so good at boxing?
He had an excellent right hook!

What does the pirate captain keep up his sleevie?
His armie.

Why was the pirate so irate?
He needed a p !

Why do pirates take so long to learn the alphabet?
They are always getting stuck at C.

How much was the pirate's treasure worth?
An arm and a leg.

What are pirates really good at?
Aaaart!

Where do you find a pirate who has lost his wooden legs?
Right where ye left him!

What do pirates wear in the winter?
Long Johns!

Why are pirates called pirates?
Because they aaaarrrrr!

What lies on the ocean floor and twitches?
A nervous wreck.

Why couldn't the pirates play cards?
Because The Captain was standing on the deck.

What did the pirate order in the restaurant?
Pizzas of eight

Why didn't the pirate's phone work?
He left it off the hook!

Why do Pirates always shop on Black Friday?
They like a good 'sail' !

Why are pirates fantastic singers.
They always hit the high Cs.

How much do pirates pay for their piercings?
A buck-an-ear.

What's a pirate's favourite kind of fish?
A swordfish!

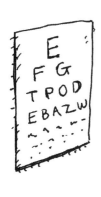

Why did the pirate visit the opticians?
*He needed an **aye** exam!*

What's a pirates favourite fish dinner?
Pieces of skate!

What vegetable should you never take to sea?
A leek!

Where do pirates get their hooks?
At the aaardware store!

Crazy World

What type of fish goes brrr um brrrum bruumm?
A motor pike!

Have I told you the story about the electric fence?
'I can't tell you - It's too much of shocker!'

Why are brooms always late?
They over-sweep!

How do you make milkshake?
'Shout Boo! at a cow!'

Have I told you the story about the very tall wall?
'I'd tell you but you wont get over it!'

Why was the alien throwing plates out of the window?
He liked flying saucers!

Why was the spy hiding in bed?
He liked to work undercover!

Have I told you about the broken clothes rail?
'I would but you wont get the hang of it.'

How does the solar system organize party?
They planet!

What do you get when you cross a shark with a cow?
I've no idea - but I wouldn't try milking it.

What do you call a dog wearing two jumpers?
A hot dog!

What did the cop say to his belly?
You are under a vest!

Why are frogs always happy?
Nothing bugs them!

What are romantic volcanoes always telling each other?
'I lava you.'

Where do bees like to sit?
On their bee-hinds!

What do you get when you cross a cheetah with a burger?
Fast food.

What do elves learn in school?
The elf-abet.

At what time of year do you see rabbits on trampolines?
Spring time.

What do you call a lazy young kangaroo?
A pouch potato.

Why was the little dog always laughing?
It was a Chi-ha-ha!

Why did the man fall in the well?
Because he couldn't see that well.

I was going to swap my brain.
What happened?
I changed my mind.

What books do meteors like to read?
Comet books!

Why should you sit in a corner when it gets cold?
Because most corners are 90 degrees.

What do snowmen eat for lunch?
Icebergers

What do you get if you cross a millipede with a parrot?
A walkie-talkie!

Why didn't the fish score any goals at the football match?
He was afraid of the net!

Why didn't the skeleton cross the road?
He didn't have the guts.

Why did the dinosaur cross the road?
Because chickens hadn't evolved yet!

Why did the worker get fired from the calendar factory.
He took a day off.

What does a snail say on a skateboard?
Wheeee!!!

Why was 6 afraid of 7?
Because 7, 8, 9!

What do you call a boomerang that doesn't come back?
A stick!

What does bread do on holiday?
Loaf around.

What time do ducks wake up?
The quack of dawn.

What's green and can fly?
Super Pickle!

What do you call a kangaroo at the North Pole?
Lost.

What's worse than finding a caterpillar in your apple?
Finding half a caterpillar!

Why do you never see elephants hiding in trees?
Because they're really good at it!

What did one eye say to the other eye?
Something smells between us!

What did the architect ask the builder?
House it going?

What kind of shoes do robbers wear?
Sneakers.

Knock, knock

Who's there?
Cargo.
Cargo who?
Car go Beep! Beep!

What do you call a woman who crawls up walls
Ivy

Have you tried archery blindfolded
No. Why would I?
You don't know what you're missing

What's invisible and smells like carrots?
Bunny Farts!
Rabbit farts!

What's brown and sticky?
A stick.

Doctors

Doctor, doctor, I think I'm invisible.
'Who said that?'

Doctor, doctor, I keep thinking people are ignoring me
'Next please!'

Doctor, doctor, I think I'm a fish.
You poor sole.

Doctor, doctor, I keep thinking I'm a pack of card
'Don't worry I'll deal with you later.

Doctor, doctor, I think I'm a pair of curtains.
'Pull yourself together sir.'

Nurse is Dr. Hedges around?
No, Dr. Hedges is tall and slim!

Doctor, doctor, I'm suffering from Déjà vu
'You told me that last time!'

Doctor I can predict the future
When did this start?
Last Wednesday!

Doctor, doctor, I'm shrinking!
'Let's be a little patient then shall we sir!'

Doctor, my pet pigs got a rash.
Don't worry, give him this oinkment!

Doctor, doctor, I feel like a pair of wigwam
You're too tense sir

Why was the doctor so short tempered?
He didn't have enough patients!

Doctor, doctor, I've swallowed a clock
Don't be alarmed sir

Doctor, doctor, I think I need glasses
I agree, this is a supermarket sir!

Doctor, doctor, I'm boiling hot!
'Just simmer down!'

Doctor, doctor, I think I'm a lampshade.
Oh lighten up!

Doctor, doctor, I think I'm a wind turbine.
Why have you come to see me?
I'm your biggest fan!

Doctor, doctor, I've hurt my arm in several places
Well don't go there anymore

Why did the unwell shoe go to the hospital?
It wanted to be heeled

Doctor, doctor, I've got bananas growing out of my ears.
When did this first start to happen?
Sorry I cant hear you, I've got bananas growing out of my ears...

Doctor it hurts when I lift my arm up.
Don't do it then!

Why did the Dalmatian dog go to the eye doctor?
Because he kept seeing spots.

Doctor, doctor, I keep hearing an annoying buzzing sound.

"Don't worry; its just a small bug that's going around."

Doctor, doctor, birthday cake gives me heartburn

Next time, take the candles off first.

Why did the banana go to the doctor?

Because it wasn't peeling well.

Doctor, doctor, birthday cake gives me heartburn.
Next time, take the candles off first.

Doctor, will I be able to play the piano after the operation?
Yes, I should think so.
That's great! I never could before!

Doctor, Doctor, will this cream get rid of my spots?
I never make rash promises.

79

Doctor, Doctor I think I'm a bell?
Go home and relax. If that doesn't help then give me a ring!

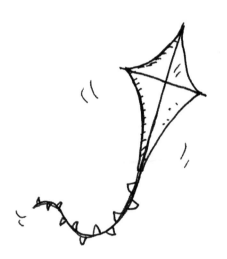

Doctor, Doctor I've got wind!
Can you give me something?
Yes, a kite!

Knock! Knock!

Knock! Knock!
Who's there?
Honey bee.
Honey bee who?
Honey bee a dear and open the door!

Knock! Knock!
Who's there?
Ken
Ken who?
Ken I come in? It's cold out here.

Knock! Knock!
Who's there?
Bella.
Bella who?
Bella not working, that's why I'm knocking!

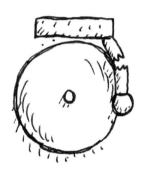

Knock! Knock!
Who's there?
Deja.
Deja who?
Knock! Knock!

Knock! Knock!
Who's there?
Voodoo.
Voodoo who?
Voodoo you think you are, asking all these questions?

Knock! Knock!
Who's there?
Interrupting cow.
Interru-
Mooooooooooo!

Knock! Knock!
Who's there?
Dozen.
Dozen who?
Dozen anyone have a key?

Knock! Knock!
Who's there?
Just
Just who?
Just passing so thought I would knock on your door!

Knock! Knock!
Who's there?
Amos.
Amos who?
A mosquito.

Knock! Knock!
Who's there?
Clare.
Clare who?
Clare the way, I'm coming through!

Knock! Knock!
Who's there?
Needa.
Needa who?
Needa hand opening the door?

Knock! Knock!
Who's there?
Mikey
Mikey who?
Mikey wont open the door!

Knock! Knock!
Who's there?
Ivor...
Ivor who?
Ivor told you before, I'm not telling you again!

Knock! Knock!
Who's there?
Figs.
Figs who?
Figs the doorbell, it's broken!

Knock! Knock!
Who's there?
Tank.
Tank who?
And thank you too!

Knock! Knock!
Who's there?
Owls
Owls who?
Yes, owls do hoo.

Knock! Knock!
Who's there?
Wooden shoe.
Wooden shoe, who?
Wooden shoe like to know!

Knock! Knock!
Who's there?
Canoe.
Canoe who?
Canoe open the door please?

Knock! Knock!
Who's there?
The Doctor.
Doctor who?
No just the doctor!

Knock! Knock!
Who's there?
Nanna.
Nanna who?
Nanna your business!

Knock! Knock!
Who's there?
Police
Police who?
Police open the door, it's cold outside!

Knock! Knock!
Who's there?
Alpaca.
Alpaca who?
Alpaca the food, lets have a picnic!

Knock! Knock!
Who's there?
Jess
Jess who?
Jess open the door and find out!

Knock! Knock!
Who's there?
Chester.
Chester who?
Chester me trying to get in!

Knock! Knock!
Who's there?
Wendy.
Wendy who?
Wendy bell works again, I'll stop knocking!

Knock! Knock!
Who's there?
Spell
Spell who?
W-H-O

Knock, knock.
Who's there?
Olive.
Olive, who?
Olive you, and I don't care who knows it.

Knock! Knock!
Who's there?
Luke.
Luke who?
Luke through the keyhole and you'll see!

Knock! Knock!
Who's there?
Candice.
Candice who?
Candice door open, or are you stuck inside?

Knock! Knock!
Who's there?
Paul.
Paul who?
Paul open the door and I'll tell you!

Knock! Knock!
Who's there?
Yul.
Yul who?
Yul find out if you open the door!

Knock! Knock!
Who's there?
Leaf
Leaf Who?
Leaf me alone!

Knock knock.
Who's there?
Stopwatch.
Stopwatch who?
Stopwatch you're doing and open the door!

Knock! Knock!
Who's there?
Wee Will
Wee Will who?
Wee Will, Wee Will rock you!

Knock! Knock!
Who's there?
Donut.
Donut who?
Donut ask me, I just got here.

Knock knock
Who's there?
I'm outstanding.
I'm outstanding who?
I'm outstanding in the rain! Let me in!

School

Why did the music teacher climb up a stepladder?
To reach the higher notes!

Where was the Magna Carta signed?
At the bottom!

Why did the student throw his watch out of the school window?
He wanted the time to fly.

Who designed King Arthur's round table?
Sir Cumference

Why did the boy eat his homework?
Because he didn't have a dog!

Why did the other boy eat his homework?
Because his teacher said it was a piece of cake!

Which Roman leader suffered from hayfever?
Julius Sneezer!

eacher: Simon, can you say your name
ackwards?
imon: *No Mis.*

Why did the lunchroom clock run slow?
It always went back four seconds!

eacher: I've got 10 bananas in this hand and
another 12 bananas in my other hand.
What have I got?
oy: *Big hands?*

Why did the teacher wear sunglasses to school?
Her students were very bright!

Why did the atom leave the science class?
It was time to split!

What's a math teacher's favourite dessert?
Pi !

What did the pen say to the pencil?
So, what's your point!

Knock Knock!
Who's there?
Dewey.
Dewey who?
Dewey have to go to school today?

Teacher: "Make me a sentence with the word lettuce."
Cheeky Lad: *"Lettuce out of school early!"*

Teacher: Who built the ark?
Pupil: *I have Noah idea!*

Which snakes are good at maths
Adders!

Why don't they do school exams in the jungle
There are too many cheetahs

Why did the giraffe fail his exams?
He had his head in the clouds.

What did the gorilla study in school?
Its Ape B C's.

Knock, knock!
Who's There?
Anita.
Anita who?
Anita to borrow a pen!

How do you make fire with just two sticks?
Make sure one of them is a match.

Where do kids learn to make ice cream?
In sundae school!

Why did the Cyclops retire from teaching?
Because he only had one pupil!

I would tell you the story about the broken pencil
But its pretty pointless

Why were the middle ages called the dark ages?
Because there was a lot of knights!

Why did the teacher jiggle her eyes
She couldn't control her pupils

ow was the Roman Empire divided?
ith a pair of Caesars!

Knock, knock!
Who's there?
Rita.
Rita who?
Rita book, you might learn something!

Who designed Noah's ark?
An ark-itect.

Who is king of the classroom?
The ruler!

Why did the students study in a hot air ballon?
Because they wanted higher grades.

What did the snake learn in school
Hissssss-tory

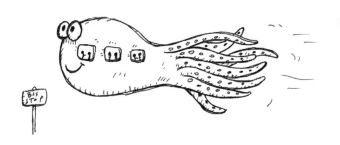

What bus wont get you to school?
An octobus!

Christmas Jokes

What did one snowman say to the other snowman?
Do you smell carrots?

Why should you never eat Christmas decorations?
You'll catch tinsellitis!

Why did the turkey cross the road?
T he chicken was on holiday!

Why is Santa always so jolly
He's blessed with good el

Where do snowmen go to dance?
Snowballs!

How does Santa tend his garden
With a Ho, Ho, Ho

Knock-Knock!
Who's there?
Mary and Abbie!
Mary and Abbie who?
Mary Christmas and a Abbie New Year!

What do elves do after school?
They do their gnome work.

What did one Angel say to the other?
Halo there!

Where does Father Christmas keep his money?
The snowbank!

Knock knock!
Who's there?
Hanna
Hanna who?
Hanna partridge in a pear tree!

Why was the Snowman kicked out of the grocery
store?
They caught him trying to pick his nose!

What expenses does Santa have to pay?
Jingle Bills!

What is a snowman's favourite drink?
Iced Tea!

What do you call a festive beach crab?
Sandy Claws!

What do ghosts like watching in the theatre?
The phanto-mines!

What do elves like baking?
Fairy cakes!

Why did Santa confiscate the elves camera?
They were taking too many Elfies!

What do snowmen like to do at the weekend
Ch

Which of Santa's reindeers has bad manners?
RUDE-olph!

What do you get when you cross a snowman with a vampire?

Frostbite!

Why wasn't the Christmas turkey hungry?

It was already stuffed!

What music do elf's listen to when working?

Wrap music!

What do you call an elf who wears earmuffs?
Anything you want! He can't hear you!

Elf 1: **Where does Mrs Clause come from?**
Elf 2: *Alaska?*
Elf 1: **Don't worry I'll ask her myself!**

How does Rudolph know its Christmas
He looks at the calen-deer

Who hides in the kitchen at Christmas?
A mince spy!

What's red and white and moving fast?
Santa skiing down a mountain!

What's Father Christmas dog called?
Santa paws

What did the snowman put on his dinner?
Chilly sauce!

How do you know when an elf has past his driving test ?
His car has NO-EL plates.

What do you get if you cross a Christmas cracker with a duck?
A Christmas Quacker

Knock! Knock!
Who's there?
Yule log.
Yule log who?
Yule log the door after you let me in, won't you?

Knock! Knock!
Who's there?
Snow.
Snow who?
Snow use. I forgot my name again!

Movies, Music & TV

Why didn't Godzilla eat the furniture store?
He was trying to cut down on suites!

What happened when Batman didn't pay his electric bill?
He had a dark knight!

Two TV aerials fell in love and got married
The wedding was dull but the reception was amazing

What does Tony Stark eat for breakfast?
Iron Bran!

Why does Dr Who smell of herbs?
Because he travels in Thyme!

What kind of music are balloons afraid of?
Pop Music

Why is Peter Pan always flying about?
He Neverlands!

bought a Television set that had broken
peakers. It was a bargain at only £5.00.
just couldn't turn it down!

Why can't Superman defeat Dracula?
He's afraid to go into the crypt at night!

Why doesn't Kermit the frog have any clothes?

He lost them in the croakroom!

Why can't you give Elsa a balloon?
Because she will Let it go

Knock, knock!
Who's there?
Art.
Art Who?
R2-D2

Why did the angry Jedi cross the road?
To get to the Dark Side.

Why couldn't Batman go fishing?
Because Robin ate all the worms!

Why did the vampire become a actor?
He wanted a part to get his teeth into.

What did the Tin Man say when he was run over by a steamroller?
'oiled again!'

What kind of car does a Jedi drive?
A Toy Yoda.

Knock, knock

Who's there?
Maida
Maida who?
Maida force be with you!

How do you make a bandstand
Take away their chair

What happened when Mr. Bean went shopping for camouflage trousers?
He couldn't find any!

Why is Yoda such a good gardener?
He has green fingers.

What do you get if you drop a piano down a mineshaft?

A-flat minor.

ow do you get Pikachu onto a bus?

ou Pokemon!

What did Arnold Schwarzenegger say when he was invited to the music themed fancy dress party?

'I'll be Bach!'

How do you fix a broken tuba?
With a tuba glue.

What do you get if you lock a cow in the Tardis
Dr. Mo

What did the baby corn say to its mother?
Where's popcorn?

How does Batman's mother call him into eat
Dinner Dinner Dinner Dinner Batman

hat was Spider man doing on his computer?
rfing the web!

What does Batgirl wear to bed?
Her Dark Knight gown!

/hy couldn't Robin see Batman dancing at the isco?
was a Dark Knight Club!

Have you heard about that new Wookie bubble gum?
It's really Chewy!

Thank you for buying this book
We hope you enjoyed it.

We sell our books on Amazon & eBay

www.retrokidbooks.co.uk

Twitter: @joketasticjokes
Redbubble: Joketastic.redbubble.com

Printed in Great Britain
by Amazon

59527027R00078